Text and illustrations copyright 2020 Akili Neer

Illustrations copyright 2020 Akili Neer

Published in 2020 by Akili Neer

All rights reserved. No portion of this book may be reproduced,

stored in a retrieval system, or transmitted in any form or by any means,

mechanical, electronic, photocopying, recording, or otherwise,

without the written permission from the publisher.

Dedicated to the unicorns in my life: my children Korah, Rivkah, & Aryeh and my husband, David. Thank you for the inspiration and encouragement. And a special thanks to all my Kickstarter backers, without whom this book would not have come to fruition.

I Wish I Were a Unicorn

by A.K. Neer

On a street like yours, not far away,
in a home that's quite the same,
there lives a child that's just like you,
who even shares your name.

Standing at the mirror, wearing wings and a horn, this child's great desire is to be a *unicorn*.

"*I wish I were a unicorn!*"
Mom heard, while passing by.
She stopped and poked her head inside,
and asked a musing, "Why?"

"I'd be so very awesome! Such a brilliant unicorn! Spectacular and magical, empowered by my horn."

"I'd have such **great adventures** soaring freely through the sky.

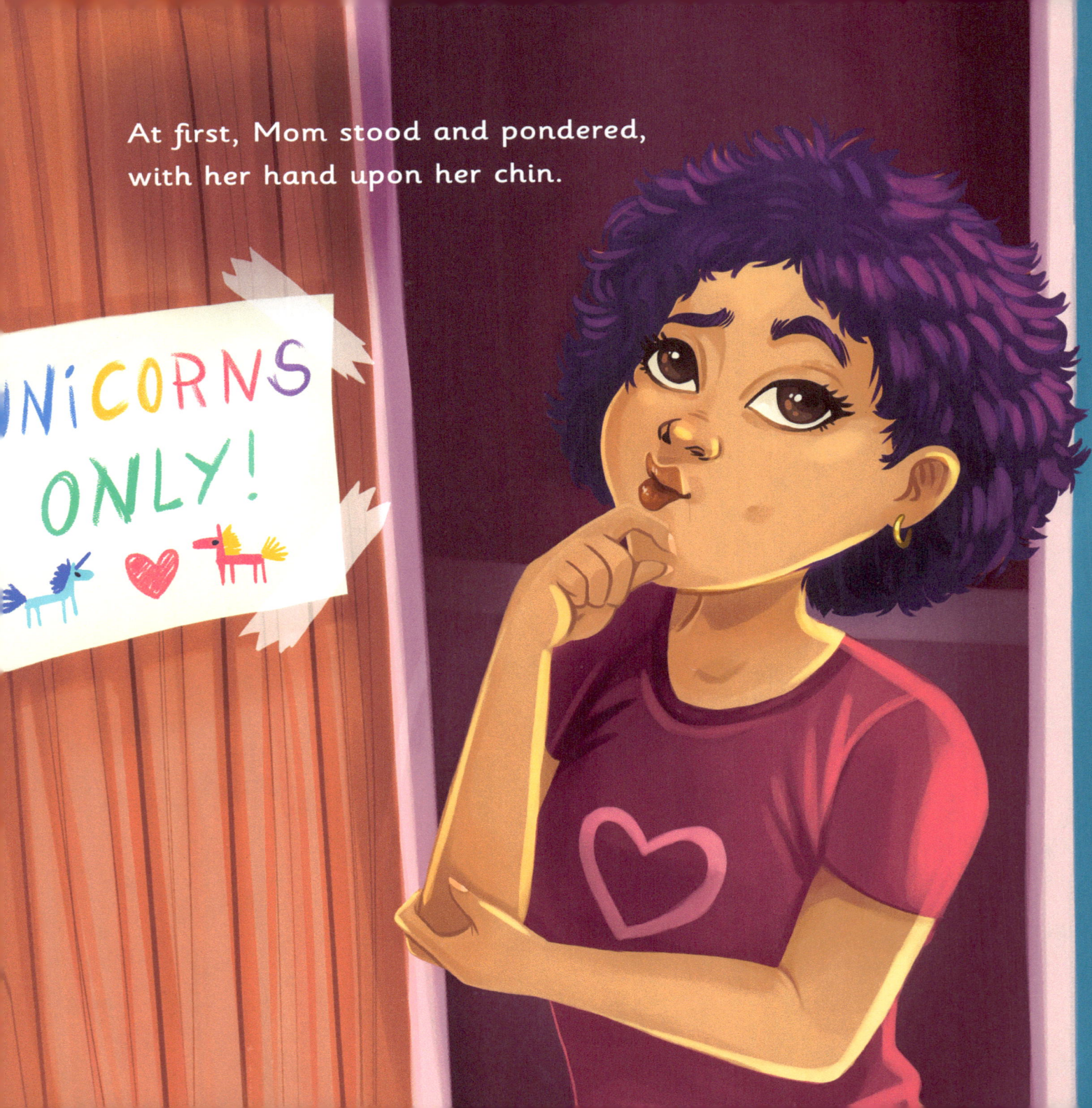

At first, Mom stood and pondered, with her hand upon her chin.

"But how?" her child inquired.
The reflection had remained.
The wings and horn, so dearly worn,
were still just plastic and plain.

"You may not have a magic horn protruding from your head,

but

magic

lies within your heart
and comes from there, instead."

And every *gentle* word you speak shows others that you care."

"Your life's a grand adventure that is waiting to unfold. Be *brave* in your endeavors, be discerning, and be *bold*."

MANY PATHS

DARK PLACES

When Mom had finished talking, and the words had settled in, a peek at the reflection showed *the unicorn within.*

That gaze into the mirror showed a magic once concealed.

A **confidence** and **knowing,** all brilliantly revealed.

Aglow with new awareness, now this child who's just like you can say with utmost certainty, *"Yes, I can see it too!"*

"I am **unique,** and I am **rare.** I know this to be true. I really ***am*** a unicorn!

And so, indeed, are *you*."

about the author

A.K. Neer is passionate about writing and producing books that include diverse characters with stories that encourage and empower young readers to know, accept, and be themselves. Inspired by her own children, she hopes her books will bring awareness of emotional intelligence to readers of all ages.

When not writing, she's a parent to three awesome children, partner to a very supportive husband, and pack leader of a precocious young Sheepadoodle. Residing in the suburbs of Atlanta, she and her family enjoy outdoor adventures, indoor boardgames, all things artistic, and being their weird, authentic selves.

about the illustrator

Natasza Remesz is a children's book illustrator focused on important topics such as mindfulness, tolerance, and acceptance. She illustrates for authors who encourage children to be happy, but also to better themselves. She always creates with the goal that her art will bring joy, hope, and inspiration for all audiences. Born and raised in Poland, she now travels through Europe, loves to dance at every free moment, and enjoys life to the fullest.

CPSIA information can be obtained
at www.ICGtesting.com
Printed in the USA
LVHW072346090622
720901LV00002B/47